Agony Uncle in China

ISBN: 1-4505-1976-8
ISBN-13: 9781450519762

Agony Uncle in China

Lessons from a Young Generation

Ralph Jennings

2010

Introduction

China: Welcome to the country that never quits changing through revolution, economic transformation and collective ambition. Chinese civilization is about 5,000 years old. So it must be hanging onto something centrifugal as it bounces, explodes and recedes through the present. So it does. China's changes, especially social ones, are while dramatic, also unconvincing and awkward.

Its young generation knows that best.

Chinese parents over fifty generally follow Confucian social values. They expect a "yes" to all requests of their children of any age. Common requests include marrying early but not in college, bearing a child within a few years of that marriage, finding stable government work near home and taking care of *them* whenever they're old or poor. They never predicted China's phoenix-like rise from a nation of squalid farm and factory encampments to one of economic boomtowns dripping in foreign investment and local startups headed for international fame. No one quite imagined monthly salaries of 5,000 to 10,000 RMB, up from the old norm of 1,500 to 2,000 RMB. (Seven RMB equal about one U.S. dollar.) Who would have thought that developed countries, which once barred Chinese nationals on fear of visa overstays, would suddenly start recruiting them as eager-to-pay graduate students?

Urban China has moved over the past ten years thanks to private industry, corruption opportunities and the country's foreign investment. Because they've made some money themselves and trust in a wealthy future, some parents encourage their children to break from the conform-or-die past—their safe zone—and do whatever they like. Contrast that with less certain or simply less fortunate families, such as most of those in the hugely populated countryside, who can't even afford health care and expect a child's future earnings to prop up two, six, ten or more struggling relatives. Their mandate: do whatever you can to make a lot of money already; and to be safe, it's better to follow old rules over new ones that we don't quite understand yet.

Most city dwellers under thirty have no siblings, as China's one-child rules, which took effect in 1979, hold strong, despite some liberalization. As a result, younger urban Chinese are often spoiled at home, vain or shy outside of it and unprepared for give-and-take in their relationships with peers.

These adult children collide in classes, in dorms and on entry-level jobs, and some of the conflicts will eat at them for years. But they are united broadly by a recent lack of Maoist chaos, a hallmark of the 1960s, or hardcore Marxist ideology, which has eased since the 1980s, though they have pushed nationalism to new highs. Young and without the memories of modern history, they quickly embrace the economic and social changes that their parents keep at a safe, suspicious distance.

Letters seeking advice anchor *Agony Uncle in China*. I began receiving them in 2000 when I took over the Just Ask advice column for 21st Century, a Beijing-based, English-language weekly circulated to students throughout China, where study of the West's flagship language is as precious as money. I would get one to fifteen letters per week, totaling about 1,500 since mid-2000. I had no advice expertise and was given none to write the column. Pick one or two interesting letters per week and write conventional responses that reflect mainstream thinking in the United States, the *21st Century* editors told me. I focused on the ones depicting trends to which large numbers of readers could relate. I prioritized those written in solid rather than sloppy English, which was about every writer's second language, to make sure I understood the point of each question. I tweaked the letters liberally to increase clarity and follow rules of grammar. In the column's early years, most people would send paper letters, so I could tell by the postmarks where they came from and would note the sender's province or municipality in my columns. Over the past few years, the questions come "via e-mail." Replies in this book, most of which were published in *21st Century* and a few of which sent privately, are in no way professional, though I tried to be encouraging and practical. I have included my replies, some of which I self-edited for clarity, in the book to advance the mini-analysis that goes with each chapter.

These letters offer a peek into China's young generation, which will shape the country and its relations with the world one day.

SECTION ONE

1. What am I supposed to do with my life?

Chinese parents who lack the temptations of bars, Christmas or Internet chats assume their late-teen children attend every class and study to justify tuition that the family might have saved for a decade. Elders set rigid study rules, flustering as their classmates put the books aside to win school elections. When it's time to seek work after college, Mom and Dad insist: stable state job with a decent income and close to home, please, unless we can come up with more money to send you abroad for advanced study, which means a better-paid, more stable job after you return to China. University students learn from one another, or from the Internet, that they should seek more interesting and higher paid work at China-based foreign firms, which are not necessarily stable and probably not near home. The result: total confusion.

An urge to break away from the habits of home can start early and come on hard:

Dear Ralph,

I'm an introverted girl. For nine years my parents and my teachers have been arranging everything for me. I hardly have done anything alone. Now I have entered a university, and I have to be independent. I need to arrange my life and study alone. Nobody tells me what I shall do and shall not do and nobody guides me to study in such detail as in high school anymore. What's worse, I can't even set for myself a clear goal. My life is in a mess and I feel lost. Moreover, I have totally lost my confidence. I can't do a single thing successfully. I've been rejected in elections every time; I failed in the translation competition and I can't communicate well enough with others. It seems I only know what books have taught me, and that's not enough. People say that one's character decides everything. I think my character just hinders me from doing a lot of things. I need your help dearly.

-Anonymous, via e-mail
March 2009

Dear Anonymous,

Success, for most of us, takes years of effort, so don't worry about a lack of quick victories in your first years at a university. You've already done more than the average student by entering elections and contests. More importantly, you already recognize that the nearly total control that your parents took over your affairs before college now holds you back. To become better integrated on campus, ask questions of friendlier classmates.

For example, find out how the translation champion prepared for the contest. Ask how that person mixes a study schedule with advanced language mastery. Your peers, not your parents, will become your most effective guides on campus.

The parent-child split usually opens with a divide between new ambitions and old obligations:

Dear Ralph,
I am a second-year student at Shanghai Foreign Trade Institute. I should and will get a good job when I graduate in two years. My parents have been working and living in a less developed town in South China for about thirty years, and they long for the return to their hometown Shanghai. I should make every effort to realize their dream and bring them to a high standard of life here, but I hope to go with my boyfriend to study abroad to follow my own dream, which may require three or more years. During that time, I could not do anything for my family. What shall I do?
-Freda Ying, Shanghai
May 2002

Dear Freda Ying,
I see two choices. One, after graduation, delay going abroad for two or three years so you can earn enough money in Shanghai to let your parents live there. Working first would increase your chances of entering a good university abroad, as admissions and scholarship committees would see the experience as a sign of career dedication. The other choice is to go abroad right after graduation. If your parents have spent thirty years in another town, they probably can survive three more years. After you return to China, the overseas education may lead to higher-paying jobs, which would lead your parents to the higher standards of living they seek in Shanghai.

Anne sees the urgency of balancing her ambitions, but as a newcomer to choices she doesn't know how:

Dear Ralph,
I'm a second-year (university) student. I can't concentrate on studies now, because there are many activities on campus. In fact, I love life as much as reading and studying. There is another reason, which is that my major is philosophy. I don't know how to balance my major with my activities. Should I calm down or get more practice for myself? Please tell me what I should do.
-Anne, via e-mail
October 2006

Dear Anne,
Balance studies and campus activities without sacrificing either. You need high grades, but if you study without a break, your personal development may suffer from lack

of exposure to the outside world, which is driven by social connections. During exam seasons and ahead of major homework assignments, study as hard as possible. When classes are proceeding at a normal pace, and on semester breaks, devote more hours to extracurricular activities. During the lulls in study, volunteer to organize a litter pickup campaign, practice for the speech contest or pursue whatever activities interest you. You also may be able to mix studies and activities: by joining a student club, for example, dedicated to discussion of philosophy.

2. Children of traditional parents suffer a lack of confidence

Conservative parents often raise their children to study hard and be humble, helping when needed and not speaking unless spoken to first. In college those grown children sit at the fronts of classrooms, listen without comment to lectures and get scores above 90. But because they're not used to taking initiative in social situations, these students suffer quietly on the sidelines as groups of classmates chatter in class. They lie awake in their bunks when their roommates play video games after lights out or talk on the phone with a boyfriend or girlfriend until 1 a.m. Fear of embarrassment paralyzes traditional kids when they're called on in class. They neglect to build career connections before college graduation and get stuck with boring jobs because their more sociable, better connected peers get the higher-paid, higher-status ones.

A parent's long, sharp tongue can kill the obedient kid's hope of self-confidence:

Dear Ralph,

I'm a girl in senior middle school grade two (a high school sophomore). In junior middle school I did very well in my studies. But when I entered senior middle school I began to taste the bitterness of failing. A girl who was not as good as me in junior middle school surpassed me. I was very sad. My mother often scolded me. She couldn't understand me. All she knows how to do is scold and satirize me. I can't stand her, so when I return home I don't want to talk to her. She never wants to encourage me. When I do a good job, she only says, "Don't be so proud. Do you think you really did that well? Think of XXX, she did better than you." When I do something bad, she says, "What are you doing? Think of XXX, she is always better than you." I don't want to be compared! We are different persons! All she does is reduce my self-confidence. I had an open-heart talk with her. But she just said coldly, "When you grow up, you will know that I did good for you. I don't want you to be proud." Am I proud? Never. I just want to give myself confidence. You may think she is just strict with me. She isn't. She never forces me to do anything. She just thought I wasn't so good, but she never helps me. My mother was my idol. She was beautiful and intelligent. When I was young, I could tell my friends proudly, "My mother is an undergraduate!" But now she has turned into a vulgar woman. I can't communicate with her. I don't want to go near her. What should I do?

Cinderella, Shanxi
April 2002

Dear Cinderella,

First, analyze why you fell behind. Do you lack something essential, or is the girl who surpassed you an outstanding person who deserves to be ahead of just about everyone? More practically speaking, can you be No. 2 and still do well on exams and get into a good university? If she surpassed you because you study less or because you don't understand a class subject, especially if you fear your ranking will hurt your academic future, get help from a teacher. If you don't fault yourself, continue to study as always. Your mother actually may be looking out for you. How did she rank in college? What about her work performance after graduation? If she regrets any experiences, she may want you to fulfill her own dreams. This wish is common among parents not only in China. Ask your mother about her life. She may initially feel self-conscious about answering your questions, but if she knows you are asking because you care, she may gradually express herself. As relations improve, ask whether her goals or regrets affect what she wants for you. Either you'll learn something from her or decide she's useless academically and has no right to criticize your scores.

Chronic classroom stage fright, often the result of accumulated ridicule from parents, peers and even teachers, can mean more than forgetting a few lines:

Dear Ralph,

I am a freshman at Anhui University. I have been studying here for about two months. I am not a boy with too much shyness. I can make conversation easily. But when I go to the blackboard to give a talk, facing all the students in the class, I always get nervous and cannot speak well, even if I have prepared before class. Can you tell me what to do and how?
-Mao Dejun, Anhui
July 2004

Dear Mao Dejun,

You feel stage fright. Fear of making a mistake stops you from performing. All but the world's most charismatic people feel that way at some point. If you're afraid of the class reaction, such as laughter or whispers behind your back, include the audience in your lecture. Build a question-and-answer session into your speech or invite a classmate to the blackboard to help you write. Even if your presentation is only a few minutes, involving the audience will shift attention to the class as a whole and make you look confident enough not only to lead a lecture but also to control other people. Lastly, expect mistakes. If you say something wrong in class, three or four people might laugh, inciting other students to follow. In that case, you should also laugh to show you recognize the mistake but that it doesn't bother you. Then the room will go quiet again as the audience expects you to continue. That's as bad as it gets, and it's not so bad.

And it could get worse:

Dear Ralph,

I'm a freshman from the countryside. I would describe myself precisely as shy, self-conscious, quiet and timid. At least I think so. Before classmates I always appear incompetent. It seems difficult for me to do something as well as my classmates. I'm sure they are bound to laugh at me and see me as a fool. So I feel unhappy every day. In addition, I have few friends, especially females. I don't know why they don't like to talk with me. For instance, when I sit with a girl in class, we can talk to each other very well. But after class we become strangers at once. A chat doesn't make us closer, but farther apart. I am in a terrible situation. What should I do?

Liuzhi, Hebei province
May 2001

Dear Liuzhi,

Your peers, including women, probably have mixed impressions of you but I'd bet that few if any consider you a fool. To ensure that most think highly of you, change your self-image. Lots of people are shy. That in itself is nothing to worry about. Do you show any real signs of incompetence or repelling people? I'd guess that you don't but fear that you do. When you realize a lot of other people are shy, you will probably act more naturally, more casually, around classmates and sound more relaxed, giving a stronger impression of friendliness. Other people will relax around you, and your social life will brighten.

3. College roommates fight over wealth, study habits, social status

University undergraduates usually live six to eight per dorm room, sharing just about everything in that ten-square-meter space. Wealthier, more socially adept students, usually from Chinese cities, tend to control phone lines and stay up late playing computer games. They also make no excuses about excluding poorer, geekier roomies, often from China's vast countryside, from game sessions or lurid lights-out chats about the opposite sex. Wealthier students complain that poorer roommates are stubbornly quiet and that their fixation on passing exams ruins the fun of college. The quiet roommates retort that the noise robs them of the peace they need to study for a great education, seen as a chance to make real money after graduation. Chinese universities make it administratively difficult to change dorm rooms but do little to make students happy where they're randomly assigned. As only children, younger college students are not used to compromising anyway, so inevitable roommate disputes easily escalate from taunts to destructive practical jokes or silent treatment that can last for months. A typical case:

Dear Ralph,

I share a dormitory room with five classmates. Four of us have computers. I usually don't spend much time on the computer, while the three others do. That is not supposed to bother me, but they are still online with the lights on late at night. What's worse, they talk and laugh loudly at the same time, which disturbs my sleep. The other two girls who don't own computers and I have talked to them several times. But regardless of others' feelings, they do what we told them not to a few minutes ago. I don't want to fall asleep in class as they do, but I can't even take a nap in the dormitory. Maybe changing dorm rooms is a good way to solve the problem. Relations among roommates at my university are subtle (complex, unspoken), so I hesitate to take action. I don't have to be their good friend, but at least not their enemy, though this (problem) is not my fault. Furthermore, I am not sure whether another dorm room is available. Now a lack of sleep is causing me to lose focus on my lessons. Could you give some advice?

-Mariah Zhang, Beijing

Dear Mariah,

Your roommates' parents probably never disciplined them for any rude behavior. Lacking siblings, they had no competitors at home, so today they figure anything goes. But you are right to seek peace as well as a solution. Computer users outnumber non-users in your room, and since you've already aired your complaints, there's little more to say. Ask for another dorm room if you can get one. You don't need to explain why you're moving out. Buy everyone a simple meal as an upbeat farewell, so they don't question your motives for leaving. If the dorm managers have no other space for you, explain to them why you want to move. Suggest that in the future your university leaders quiz incoming students about their study habits before assigning rooms. This advice, if taken seriously, could help future generations gain the sleep that you have lost.

The typical low-rise dormitory looks like a factory block with brick walls and square windows in perfect rows and columns. Three to four bunk beds lie head to foot in every room. Each student gets a slab of wood as a desk. Roommates share a phone line and at better schools an Internet connection for whoever brings a private computer, inevitably sharing it to avoid looking elitist. Freezing winter air leaks through the windows. Air-conditioning is rare. Public restrooms along the cement-floored halls smell like students seldom aim and dorm staff seldom cleans. The buildings may face on-campus construction sites where workers hammer into the night under stadium lights that go off only at sunrise. Through these walls, twice a year, pour eighteen-year-olds from all over China, lugging cartoon-decorated toiletry bags, clothes of all price levels for all occasions, celebrity posters, the shock of leaving young lovers behind in a distant hometown and parents trailing behind with second thoughts about whether they should have splurged for an off-campus apartment. A hyper-typical case:

> *Dear Ralph,*
> *I am a college junior. These days a problem occupies my mind. On our campus, there are eight students in each dormitory room, and altogether about 450 persons in ONE building, which has caused many problems. Last term, a student was killed by one of his roommates because of disputes when playing cards. Constant cold wars in the dormitory make it stifling. Furthermore, every year we have to pay a 1,200-yuan (about 7.8 yuan to the U.S. dollar at that time) dorm fee, which is higher than other colleges under the same conditions. Sometimes I really don't want to live in such an annoying place, but I have no choice. I think this is quite unfair. As college students, we should have proper rights. But how do we get them?*
> *-Jerry, via e-mail*
> *Autumn 2003*

> *Dear Jerry,*
> *Unless you are wealthy enough to live off campus in your own apartment, stay in the dormitory and make the best of it. The dormitory itself does not cause fatal card-playing disputes or cold wars; the variety and density of students do. Reexamine your seven roommates and the guys next door. You probably consider some friends, study buddies or at least not mortal enemies. You wouldn't know them as well if you lived alone. Not everyone in*

the dorm will become your friend, but you can usually live in peace with a majority by just greeting people. If cold wars really overshadow any hope of peace, spend as much time as possible outside the dormitory, such as in the yards or cafeterias, until things improve.

When cold wars escalate anyway, expect this:

Dear Ralph,

When I entered the university, I knew relationships among people were complicated. My roommates all want higher scores than others. So when they knew I had exam review data in my MP3, they asked to borrow it, then copied the data and revised mine. I argued with them about this fiercely and later said nothing to them. I've always thought we should never play practical jokes. But perhaps they don't think so. They routinely play practical jokes on me, such as drawing pictures on my clean clothes, changing the book that I put on my desk and destroying the earrings that I've placed in my pen container. Meanwhile, they always see films and make so much noise at night that it all affects my sleep. I don't want to change my room, because that procedure is difficult at my school. I also don't want to say anything to a teacher, because I think that would be meaningless. Now I am so sad. How can I deal with this?
-June, Shanghai

Dear June,

I would normally suggest that you try to make amends to your roommates by socializing with them, gradually and cautiously, with a sense of humor, indicating that the problems don't faze you. Normally, they would return your goodwill by treating you well again. But your roommates have wrecked personal property and caused you to lose sleep; they do not sound like people willing to change. If you stay in the dorm, they might destroy more of your stuff or further disrupt your academic life. I know switching rooms can be a headache, but if you explain the issue to a dormitory manager just as you explain it here, you stand a good chance of getting an upgrade.

4. University study: major in dating; minor in video games

First-year college students, competitive and ambitious after sweating out admissions exams since middle school, may fancy the university as a theme park of top professors and stunning academic discussion with degrees automatically qualifying them for China's top jobs. But as required Marxist-Leninist political theory classes drag into junior year while professors rack up some of the highest absence rates on campus to pursue higher-paid side jobs, students get disillusioned. Then there's the poetry-perfect girl (or movie-star male) who sits across the room in study hall and the scientific fact that everyone else on campus seems to have one. Other guys are also involved in all-night computer game tournaments. Women leave campus to shop for designer mobile phones and meet moneyed off-campus men. The top players and star shoppers probably have family members who can arrange jobs after graduation, making study irrelevant. Smarter students, perhaps solitary or over-studious at first, eventually realize that these non-academic pursuits build social confidence valuable to finding career connections after the college party ends.

Joanna, first inclined to study throughout her college years, battled Internet temptations:

Dear Ralph,

I'm a college student. I was always a hard-working student in high school, but now I find that I can't put myself into study wholeheartedly. As the final exams were coming once, I was very worried about my study. Maybe I relax too much. Several months ago, I learned to surf the Internet. Soon, it became my favorite hobby. When I don't want to study, I will go to the Net bar to chat with others. I've spent too much time and money on it. Although I tried to control myself, I can't resist the temptation. When I thought that my parents had put all their hopes on me, I felt very ashamed of my action. [Parents usually pay full tuition, room and board in China.] But sometimes I just can't control myself, and I only want to find pleasure on the Internet. I'm very worried about my study and my future. Can you give me some advice?

Joanna, via e-mail
2003

Dear Joanna,
Go online only between set hours every day, leaving the rest of your time to study. That way, you'll still have the pleasure of the Net but not ignore your studies. You might find it hard initially to sign off when your time is up, but think of your parents and your grades. Remember you can go back online the next day. If the time limit doesn't work, try a task limit. For example, send e-mail to just three people, check the weather online, chat with a friend for fifteen minutes and then quit. If you still can't quit the habit, go cold turkey. Stay off the computer until your homework is done or the exam season passes. But take study breaks to drink tea, read an escapist novel or talk with friends in person. Without something to ease your information-saturated mind, it will tire out. Then you might return to the Internet.

University student Celery knew she had to strike a balance:

Dear Ralph,
I'm an undergraduate. Last year I fell in love with a boy in our department. But I don't know if he loves me. Moreover, we haven't spoken to each other. Every day we have our classes in the same classroom. So we can meet every day. Sometimes I try to be close to him, but I have not found much encouragement and I always think of my studies. I'm afraid that he can affect my studies. I think of my studying as the most important thing. To my disappointment, I can't help thinking of him when I study or when I'm in bed. I don't know how to balance my studies and my feelings. I hope you can help me.
Celery, via e-mail
September 2002

Dear Celery,
Boy-girl attractions are normal at school. You will naturally think of your classmate as you study and think of your studies when you are around him, especially if relations pick up. If you discipline yourself to pursue both study and the boy by setting up special times for each, you can have both without losing a grip on either. But since the boy has not made anything clear to you yet, you should either forget him, focusing entirely on studies, or express your interest in him. Otherwise you'll be absorbed not by the boy but by confusion.

College student Figoll-211 had already half-exterminated his studies:

Dear Ralph,
I'm a freshman English major in Guangxi. My hobby is "Half-Life," one of the most popular computer games about battles in China. But my problem is that there is a contradiction with my study. In fact, I have sworn a thousand times to quit this game, but every time my roommates ask me to play, I do it without hesitation. However, when I come out of the computer club, I always regret it and promise: I won't go there. But eventually I break my promise again! College costs my parents a lot of money. I have had a sense that I owe my parents from the time I was born till today. So I don't owe them anything in the future,

I have to study hard to earn more money to show I was worth spending money on, and to repay my parents. When I was a child, I had the aim of being a businessman, but how can I achieve my ambition if I behave like this? The computer games are just like a drug. It's like a snake that charms you and gives you poison if you don't give up immediately. My room-mates and I have established a team, named "King Team of 211." I am the leader. Should I disband this team and study or play this game twice a week?

Figoll-211, Guangxi
May 2002

Dear Figoll-211,
Don't quit the game. Just control the number of hours you play. A lot of computer games have a snake-like attraction, but not all players become addicts. People with self-discipline can become routine players who also do well in school or at work. On the study side of your contradiction, ask yourself honestly whether you're interested in classes. Do you attend them? Do you study after class, and if so, do you look forward to it? Think about how you could be charmed into studying harder. If possible, pick courses that you like and find a persuasive study buddy. Pressure to repay parents, however real, is an incentive but hardly a charm. Something else: The side of your mind that makes you good at a battle game might also make you a top business management student.

5. Dating: Know the rules first

Dating in China is a brief intro to marriage, which is a required rite around age twenty-five. Marriage means money because China is poor and one can't depend on people outside the family. Young adults give their parents the final word in picking a spouse: usually a well-studied man with access to money or a task-conscious woman willing to take care of elders. So goes the rulebook according to most Chinese people over forty and of nearly all ages in the countryside. But city dwellers these days are telling their middle-aged parents there's a revised edition out: It describes dating as a way to meet lots of prospective mates. Girls with supersized eyes and gumdrop mouths and super-confident bad boys who prefer basketball or punk rock to studies top the prospect list. Selection per the revised rules can last from one's teens through late thirties. Mom and Dad can vote on the eventual spouse, but hold no veto power.

A showdown might start before a suitor even shows up:

Dear Ralph,

I'm twenty-five years old. I'm a tall and good-looking girl. My salary is also not bad for my city. To my parents, I'm old enough to marry. I still do not have a boyfriend. (I had a boyfriend last year. We said goodbye after I realized we really did not love each other.) So they are anxious to push me to find a good man. Most of my friends and classmates are going to marry or already have. But I have not found the man who loves me and who I love. Sometimes I intend to find a future husband through a matchmaker. I'm afraid of the pressure from family and society. What should I do?

-Helena, via e-mail
December 2002

Dear Helena,

An ideal marriage lasts for life, so don't marry only because of pressure. If you choose someone out of panic, you may forget to take the time to evaluate your choice. Some people mistake love for fast-forming attraction, get married and then realize there's no love. Real love takes time. Other people, especially those who use matchmakers, find potential mates who look good on the surface, but it takes time to know whether someone, despite his list of achievements, will get along with you every day for the next few decades. To handle society's pressure, explain that you are actively searching for men, but don't choose a husband until you're sure you like the choice.

Parents tend to get impatient around Helena's age. But before then, beaus are often verboten:

Dear Ralph,
I am a college student from a village. It is hard for my parents to support my college study, so I made up my mind to work hard in college. My mother forbids me from loving boys, and I promised I wouldn't seek boyfriends. In the first term on campus, I made several male friends but no boyfriends. I get on well with them. I seek nothing except friendship. But these days one of the boys has expressed love to me. I've become nervous. Frankly speaking, I am afraid, because I don't want to waste time. However, I get on well with him. I don't know how to refuse him. It's my fault. I don't have a strong will. I find I have fallen in love with him. But I still remember my promise and my mother's words. I don't know how to deal with it.
-Sad Bird, Hangzhou
May 2001

Dear Sad Bird,
It's a myth that dating threatens academic success. Lots of Americans study, work part-time to pay tuition and go on dates. Life becomes a busy mess, but people in their late teens and twenties can usually handle that. People at your age should also experiment with life's pleasures. I suggest you get to know the boy slowly, particularly on weekends, while leaving most of your time for studies. He also will probably need to study, so you could even do that together. That way you can still take good grades home to your mom on the next academic break. During the same vacation you'll also find plenty of time to get to know the boy a bit better.

College guys may worry early on about early signs of earning potential such as good grades or contest victories:

Dear Ralph,
I'm a new student at a university. In our class I see a girl who is very beautiful. And I find that many characteristics of hers are like mine. At the beginning I wanted her to become my girlfriend. But I haven't had any achievements, so I got rid of my idea to pursue her. Do you think I'm right?
-ND, Shanxi
November 2001

Dear ND,
You're wrong. Finding a girlfriend isn't like getting admitted to a university. You don't need "achievements." Just go ask her out.

ND might be compatible with Ingrid Zheng, if not for her parents:

Dear Ralph,

This year I turned twenty-six, which in my city is an ought-to-marry age. So I'm extremely confused, as there are two paths in front of me. One is, according to my parents' wish, to marry a university teacher who has a rather stable job, salary and house. The other is my own will. I have been in love with a boy who works in another city far away from mine. He hasn't got a stable job or salary, and he hasn't bought a home. I think he'll own everything in the future. But my parents, relatives and friends are all against our contact.

-Ingrid Zheng, Hubei
March 2002

Dear Ingrid Zheng,

If you don't like the university teacher, forget him. If possible, move to where the other guy lives, especially if you're sure about your future with him. If you married the teacher, your parents would be happy, and you might grow to be that way as well. But his stable job, salary and house do not guarantee that happiness. You'd need to know him better. Same for the boy who you like: make sure by getting to know him well that he can really offer the love you imagine. If you choose this boy, plan how to explain your decision to doubtful friends or relatives. Tell them why you think the man you prefer will find a stable job, salary and home. Tell them why you prefer him to the teacher. Arrange for him to meet your family.

Elders keen on the practical side of marriage might approve of the next scenario, but Felix explains why it wouldn't work:

Dear Ralph,

I'm a female university sophomore and recently find myself emotionally disturbed by a subtle feeling towards one of our teachers. He has just finished his master's degree at the age of about twenty-eight. Though he hasn't yet had a girlfriend, I feel it impossible to establish a relationship between us. Students are without a doubt subordinate to their teachers. I know crystal clear that a woman in love with her boss will be very passive and miserable, but that she just can't help it. A person blinded by love can act quite irrationally and make irretrievable mistakes. Certainly I don't want to see myself fall into this category. Can you help me?

Felix, via e-mail
March 2003

Dear Felix,

You know this teacher only in class, a stage for his knowledge and leadership skills rather than for his full personality. He knows you no better than you know him. Women with subtle feelings toward their bosses mistakenly fancy them as capable, benevolent father figures. Those impressions probably differ from what a woman would discover about the same man through dates, phone calls and other one-on-one interaction. Contact with the teacher outside class would show you who he really is. But as you say, dating an authority figure invites status-gap conflicts, which could stunt communication or create an unwelcome father-child relationship. Good teachers also shun dates with students to avoid perceptions in class of inappropriate preferential treatment. Since you describe your feeling toward the teacher as "subtle," I doubt you are blinded yet by love. While you can still see, look around for men of your own status who you can get to know one on one.

6. Real people suck. Everyone's a hero online

Online dating has replaced nights out for a lot of young Chinese since the Internet took off in 2000. Women use chat rooms, instant messengers, Facebook or plain e-mail to pursue fantasy romances consistent with the movies. Some avoid meeting the guy behind the dialogue box in case he spoils the fantasy by ordering cheap food on dates or getting nervous when he talks. They'd hate to find out that he's fifty-five instead of twenty-five as he claims. Shy men get to know women online to avoid the shifty eyes or blushes that might mar a face-to-face first date. Both sides can script perfect lines before hitting "send." They upload only their best digital self-portraits, perhaps from five or ten years ago. Emoticons work when portraits fail. Online dating can last through the run-up to marriage, which I suspect was on Maggie's mind.

Dear Ralph,

I am a third-year university student. I have a boyfriend from California. We met via Internet messenger and chatted for about half a year. He is working as a musician and a part-time doctor. We have seen each other's photos. He is very thoughtful and has said he loves me very much. He will come to Hong Kong this April and may see me. I am glad, but still worry as my English is limited and I can't express myself very well. Also, what if the culture and lifestyle are different between us? To some extent, I love him also, but I can't help worrying about the future. Should I take this love seriously?

-Maggie, via e-mail
March 2004

Dear Maggie,

A love affair needs extended face-to-face time to get serious. A meeting in Hong Kong will be a good start. But unless you live in the same city together for six months to a year, seeing him regularly, you won't know him well enough to decide whether he'd make a suitable husband. The Internet puts two people on their best, most-calculated behavior. Online you don't face real-life situations such as deciding how to spend money or dealing with third parties such as choosy or nosy parents. Sometimes the Net lies. Maybe he doesn't really look the way he appears in photos. In-person exposure will let you see how he handles moments in life as they randomly occur. Moreover, you will discover over a few months of face-to-face contact whether language and culture cramp relations.

Online dates are also easy to hide from parents who seek to screen partners or who disapprove of dating while in school. Existing beaux can't see what happens four to six hours a day on a partner's office computer, via wireless connections in college classrooms or at cyber-cafes that draw students into all-night chats.

Dear Ralph:
Four months ago, my girlfriend was infatuated with chatting on the Internet and fell in love with a boy. I got mad when I found out what happened and beat her. She just cried but said nothing. Eventually, she promised never to do it again. But after that incident, I began to distrust what she does. For example, when she works late, I'll wonder if she's really at the office or outside with another boy. This suspicion obsesses me day and night and even influences my regular study and my work. How should I do better?
  -Aaron Ye, via e-mail
  2003

Aaron,
Talk to your girlfriend instead of beating her. She has the right to communicate with whomever she wants. If you speak to her and treat her kindly, relations should naturally improve, reducing any temptation to meet other boys online or elsewhere. If you really like your girlfriend, give her time and patience. If she really likes you, she'll tell you the truth about what she's up to after work, leaving you no reason to suspect a lie.

Online dalliances can continue after marriage, as affairs are as common as computers in China:

Dear Ralph,
I graduated from a university in 2000 and married a classmate who I had loved for more than four years. But just half a year later we divorced. The main reason was that he fell in love with one of his cyber friends who he had known for only three months. After that, I still stayed in the same city, tried my best to forget the terrible memories and tried to start a new relationship with a middle-school teacher. But I failed finally. So I moved to Shenzhen (major city in southern China) last year and began a new life. However, it's not easy. I am twenty-eight and will get older and older. I am not smart, I am not beautiful and I have poor communication skills, so it's very hard for me to get to know men. I feel lonely sometimes. My parents worry about my marriage so much that I feel very strong pressure, and I am afraid of being single for the rest of my life. Although I am eager to have a serious boyfriend and build a family, I've lost my trust in love. I hate my ex-husband but still love him! I also try to forgive and let go, but it doesn't work. I want to change this unhappy state. But what can I do?
  Amanda, Shenzhen
  2005

Dear Amanda,

You don't have to forgive or forget the ex-husband. You stood by him for more than four years and probably found admirable qualities, so you naturally still feel something. How soon you stop loving him depends on what you do next. Twenty-eight is not old. Everyone defines beauty and intelligence differently; don't assume what others will think of you. Go on offline dates with guys who your friends or worried family suggest. Join clubs such as an "English corner" that promote communication with strangers. You naturally distrust love because of the divorce. But as you meet men, remind yourself that no one else is your ex-husband. Other men are unlikely to copy his exact actions. But the caution you learned from the divorce will lead you to choose the next guy carefully.

7. Entry-level workers play office politics or flee

Chinese college graduates start careers expecting to prove their worth through skills and hard work. They often discover within the first year that any praise, pay and promotions hinge largely on skill in office politics; that is, how well they satisfy the boss. After this initial disillusionment, graduates recognize please-the-boss syndrome from campus, where scholarships and class monitor positions go to students who get along best with teachers who make those decisions. Graduates who got somewhere by being sweet on their teachers quickly excel in office politics. When the real boss is absent or weak, vigilante office politicians fill the power vacuum, insisting that their peers treat them like authority. Those with less confidence quit, especially when they get word that some other company offers more prestige or even just a tiny bit more pay. Entry-level workers may rack up six to eight jobs in half as many years before realizing that they prefer school and begin applying for post-grad study. Here's how the cycle might start:

Dear Ralph,

It's time for students to get their scholarships in our school. But some of them cheated on their exams and got good results in the end to get the money. I feel that's unfair and I'm furious about this. Most of us have tried our best to learn well, but those dirty guys who got what they shouldn't get are being rewarded. I always believe this proverb: "Life is unfair, so you must get used to it!" But sometimes I can't really get used to it and even ask myself why we should. You know it's not the problem of money. It's trust. Please help me. What should I do?

-Apple Lee, Sichuan
November 2005

Dear Apple Lee,

You should be mad. Trust in the scholarship selection process, or in any system that rewards hard work, helps immensely to build a productive society. Scholarship money matters, as well. As your proverb suggests, some cheaters will use back-door means to land plum jobs and seek promotions. You will see more of these examples in school or later on the job. You must get used to it. However, by remaining honest you will win admiration from people around you who share your principles.

Eager Angelina fears she's stuck in a job where most of the staff is lazy:

Dear Ralph,

I'm a bank clerk. Frankly, the pay is good, and the work is relaxing. But I really don't like it because I feel it's too boring to bear. And the people around me have nothing to do every day but chat. So I can't learn anything from work. I want to learn some real things while I'm still young, so I've decided to seek a change. But my parents were very angry when they heard this. They thought I was almost crazy and forbade me to change my job. What should I do?

-Angelina, Shanghai
August 2001

Dear Angelina,

Quit, but not yet. First find another job that offers the same pay but more interesting work. Use your free time to look at job ads and call employers. To get a sense of whether another job would suit you better, ask revealing questions during interviews. Get a detailed job description and ask yourself whether the duties interest you. Find out about promotion prospects for top-performing workers. Finally, chat with a few would-be co-workers to see how they like the job. Do you sense enthusiasm or more laziness? If you can switch to a more rewarding job with no change in pay or status, your parents can't be angry.

A classic case of when the boss isn't really the boss:

Dear Ralph,

One of my colleagues is very arrogant and behaves like he is the boss whenever the real one is out. He is ready to teach us anything whether or not others like it. He also likes asking about private matters and making comments. Although I'm eager to learn more to improve my work ability, and although he has helped me at times, I cannot bear his boss-like manner and tone. It is said that "office politics" are complicated. I really don't know how to express my feelings to him. Sometimes I think this situation can't be changed, because he's just that kind of person as well as the one closest to our boss. I really need advice.

-Elf, Beijing
September 2005

Dear Elf,

If he's not your boss, you have a right to ignore what he says. You can say, "Sorry, I don't have time now" to make the co-worker back off without offending him. All along, be sure to do quality work that the real bosses can see. But if the problem co-worker gets along well with your bosses, he may influence the senior company leaders to punish or sideline you if you're too flippant or refuse his orders. This guy, in his weak defense, is probably exploiting your company's loose or poorly-defined management structure to live out personal dreams of power. He may assume you and other employees will respect him because he knows something or because he has seniority. If other employees treat him like a boss, his ego will swell further. So when you tell him you're too busy, keep him calm by speaking politely and supporting yourself with strong reasons.

8. Dreams, decisions and the demons that divide them

Explore the world. Study what you want. Enjoy life, as maybe we didn't. And we'll pay for it: That's the cue from newly wealthy Chinese parents to their young adult children with multi-colored hair, penchants for punk rock and degrees in the arts. Back from overseas, where they've put off full-time work for a couple of years to attend prestigious grad schools, these twenty-somethings might return to China as film producers or travel writers. But this cruise into adulthood, for most, is pure fantasy. Studious undergraduates from China's countryside, where parents often save up a child's tuition for years at the expense of their own health care, can barely afford meals with their moneyed urban classmates, let alone graduate school. No dreams allowed.

Signs of lifelong wealth gaps, promising different futures, show in college:

Dear Ralph,

I'm a freshman at a university in Nanjing. Recently, some of my roommates' parents went to see them with a lot of new clothes and food. They have also invited our whole dormitory to meals. I've attended three such meals. My parents are both (blue-collar) workers, and they hardly have holidays, even during festivals. Besides, my home is not very rich compared to those of my roommates. It would cost a lot for my family to come to my university even once. So I didn't slip even a word to my parents about the meals. But I do feel guilt, and I hope I can invite my roommates out to eat as they have invited me. What can I do?

Liu Yan, Jiangsu
November 2001

Liu Yan,

Your parents aren't obligated to treat your roommates. They work hard for the family, and that's first priority. You're right not to tell your family about the meals, sparing them needless guilt. But you don't need to be rich to return the favors of your roommates. Instead of buying a two-hundred-yuan meal, get a sack of colorful but common supermarket candy for ten yuan, for example, and leave it in the dorm room for everyone to eat. As the candy lasts for days or weeks, your roommates should remember that sack for longer than they remember any meal.

Wei Liang faces a choice between what's fun and what pays:

Dear Ralph,

I am a junior at a military academy majoring in electrical engineering. I often feel not too good. I have been worrying about this major since I entered college because I am not interested in the science of engineering at all. However, I like the arts very much. My dream is to be a writer. I often write daily entries on my blog. Only the arts can give me pleasure, I think. I cannot find the right direction in my college years. Should I give up my dream or go on with my major?

-Wei Liang, Hebei
October 2007

Dear Wei Liang,

I suspect you have pursued engineering for three years because someone, likely your parents, made you do it for the salary potential or the prestige. Whose disapproval would you face if you switched from science to arts? If you can handle the opposition, make the switch provided that the academy won't penalize you for it. If you can't change majors, continue writing in your own time. Your blog entries might eventually expand into a book, which alone could change your career focus.

Dreams come back to haunt some who ignore them:

Dear Ralph,

I graduated ten years ago. Like other Chinese children who follow in their parents' footsteps, I majored in the same field that my parents chose, and I didn't like it at all. In recent years, I've tired of the job. I have other knowledge that has nothing to do with my work, but I'm not into it. I feel lost. How can I make a decision between my career preference and what I studied in my major? How should I know what career is suitable for me?

-Rosemary, via e-mail
October 2007

Dear Rosemary,

You must experiment to find out whether the old dream is realistic. If you have education that can lead to a different career, go for it, and if you need further study, just take extra classes after work. To be safe, don't quit your present job until you find another one. After a few years of trying it, you should know whether the second career suits you. Be ready to explain the choice to your parents, who may expect you to continue duplicating their lives. Remind them that even in a field they don't know as well you can still enjoy stability and earn money.

9. Quiet or outspoken, angry youth told to shut up

Young Chinese know when they're getting shafted. A few don't mind saying so, but leaders seldom negotiate. Still, bold college students will confront teachers, usually by letter or via the dean, about lazy instruction or unfair treatment of classmates, both common practices. Teachers may snub or downgrade those who challenge them. As adults, children may quit talking to rigid or verbally abusive parents. In keeping with Confucian authority norms, parents seldom admit fault or change their ways. When entry-level workers suddenly walk off their jobs, employers explain them away as one-off malcontents. But most Chinese youth who get cheated never vent to the source. Leaders never imagine what they can't see.

Dear Ralph,

I'm a college student in civil engineering. Something happened this term that makes me very unhappy. My major teacher, a strange and strict man, is a famous engineer in my city. I didn't know more about him until the day I handed in my design work. He said my work was nothing but rubbish. I was so grieved to hear it that I didn't sleep for two days, in order to finish my work. But he only said it was rubbish and didn't even look at it carefully. I retorted that it wasn't rubbish. I thought there was nothing more to say, but my classmates told me the teacher wrote a mark under my name on his notebook. After the examination, I found I had failed in my major course. It's impossible. I studied well, reviewed carefully and did well on the examination. Some classmates who didn't study well passed. How can he do this? It's unfair. I did so much, working harder than others, but got a no-pass because I talked back to him? I look down upon the teacher, no matter how knowledgeable he is. I want a face-to-face dispute with him, but I know it's useless.

Blue, via e-mail

July 2005

Dear Blue,

It's unfair, but get used to it. Even professionals can act unprofessionally, playing favorites and degrading dissenters. Sass-back only makes a problem worse. Avoid the face-to-face dispute and do as well as you can in the class. Remember that the teacher's actions against you are not exceptional. You may find more teachers like him in later years or work for a boss who operates the same way.

Dear Ralph,

I'm a middle school student of seventeen. My school is an advanced middle school. The teachers are very educated, and I'm happy to study in such a school. But my head teacher thinks I'm a naughty, nervous student just because I quarreled with my art teacher. I'm very sorry! Every day I get a dim look from his eyes, and he doesn't ask me to answer questions any longer. In my heart I really want to tell him I'm not the kind of student he thought. In my view, a teacher should be another father or mother to the student, to love not hurt them. I don't know what I can do. I'm very anxious about it. I usually cry in the night.

Judy, Hubei Province
May 2001

Dear Judy,

Forget about the two teachers. Study as hard as possible to prove you're worthy of the school's status. After class, make friends with other students. They can offer moral support, especially if they've had similar disputes with instructors at your school. It's unlikely that you're the only student who has been slighted. By getting good grades and making friends, you'll learn that the opinions of two teachers need not ruin your self-esteem or your academic performance.

Getting cheated by a teacher prepares students for their careers:

Dear Ralph,

I'm a worker in a state-owned enterprise. I work shifts and dislike my job. But I stay here for the luxurious salary. There was once an English examination. It was the only opportunity to change my job and working conditions. I like English and never broke off English studies after graduation. Moreover, there were few workers senior to me. So I was very confident in this selective trial. But the result was unbelievable: I failed the exam. Several colleagues told me the nominee had already been designated, but I preferred to believe it was my failure. Then the name list was published. The only one selected from our shop was one of our leader's daughters. Suddenly I came to realize that I was the victim. I fell into deep sorrow. How can I face the future life in this realistic society? How can I still work in this factory? I feel hopeless. Should I leave? What can I do?

Miss Zhang, Jiangsu province
November 2001

Dear Miss Zhang,

First ask to see your exam score. The company should give you a number, just as in college. If they can't provide that detail, you have cause to suspect they lied about your failure. Also, how well does your leader's daughter write in English? Send her a note in English to see how she replies. Finally, ask colleagues or leaders to you trust whether the company evaluated only English proficiency to choose people for the job promotion. They might also have considered the quality of each applicant's routine work and on-the-job enthusiasm. If you think you will remain bitter for a long time, affecting your work, take your English skills to a better company. You say you dislike your job except for the salary anyway. On the last day at work, slip a note under the boss's door explaining what happened. Support everything you write with evidence. This final stab will make you feel good and alert the company that at least one of its employees knows that it practices favoritism.

10. Odd and extreme cases

Not every advice seeker fits the convenient chapter headings of this book.

I get occasional questions about animal rights or the wisdom of intervening in street-side disputes to help strangers. Both topics reflect advances in China's relatively new civil society, which previously put animals on a level with inanimate objects and saw helping strangers in distress as liability hazards. I learned the underlying theory from Tina:

Dear Ralph,

I am a student at Lanzhou Railway University. Nowadays, many questions confuse me. I feel that this world is so dark, full of darkness. There are so many wars and conflicts in this world. I think if people continue to do so many bad things, our world will be destroyed at last. The earth can't afford so many burdens anymore. Today many people lose themselves. They don't know their true needs. What do they really want? They just pay attention to pursuing money. Money seems so important to them. Money has closed their eyes. In my opinion, money is not important, because it can't help people find peace and truth. What do you think is more important, money or ideas? I have many, many questions.

Tina, Gansu, 2002

Dear Tina,

As American elders sometimes tell their juniors, "You can make the world a better place." They mean dedicate some of your own life to preventing conflict and destruction. No one person can change the whole world, but anyone can influence a few others, who may go on to influence a few more people, who influence some more. Suddenly your ideas are being heard. If you want to stop conflict, for example, make peace among friends when they argue, suggesting calm negotiations. If you believe ideas should supersede money, explain this viewpoint in class, during a public debate or again among friends. But prepare for disagreement, remembering that most people in China are still poor and must consider personal survival before bigger causes.

Writers occasionally send pained letters about family strife such as dragged-out divorces, drug-addicted siblings or fathers who gamble away family income. They don't know how to bring peace to their homes. Embarrassed by the lack of household harmony, they may have never discussed family issues with anyone face to face. My guess is that Kathleen hadn't told this story before:

Dear Ralph,

Seven years ago, my father changed his job and had an affair with one of his colleagues. Since then, my family has changed. Before, we were a happy family. Now my father comes back home late in the night and sometimes not at all. What's worse, he started shouting at my mother and beats her heavily. My mother has been deeply hurt. Gradually, I became a pessimistic girl of few words. Two years ago, my father changed his job again, and I thought everything was over. But a few months ago, my mother discovered that he still kept in touch with that other woman. When I came back from college, Mother told me about this. I am so disappointed. I've become deadened to what has happened around me. Right now, I really do not know what I can do to adjust myself. I want to be an optimistic girl but I always think of the miserable past. I really want to change. Would you please help me?

Kathleen, via e-mail
October 2005

Dear Kathleen,

You are innocent of whatever your father does away from home and whatever he does to your mother. But you may be able to ease tension by being a good companion to both. Ask both Mom and Dad plenty of friendly, easy questions without accusing either one of wrongdoing. Listen to their answers without judgment. If they are allowed to express themselves to you, presumably someone they trust, the dialogue could ease some of the emotional burdens that underpin the problems you describe. Over time, as they feel more at ease, your parents might be more attentive to each other as well as to you. Meanwhile, pursue your own life outside home. Dedicate yourself to studies, jobs and friends, all of which will determine your future regardless of what your parents do.

The overweight, the super-short, the very dark-skinned and others who look strikingly different in conformist China learn early about ridicule. This woman's question about her height illustrates the Chinese fixation with conformity and the habit of spotlighting outliers:

Dear Ralph,

I'm a really tall girl, 177 centimeters, far exceeding the average female height in China. As a result, I have lots of trouble almost every day. I have to struggle to get used to the strange look in the eyes of most people who I encounter. I've always wondered why no one dares to ask the weight of a fat man or woman, even though everybody wants to know about my height to fulfill a curiosity. My roommates never give up kidding me with questions such as "What's the height of your boyfriend in the future?" What's more, sometimes a boy who is shorter than me may suddenly murmur behind my back, "It's too unfair." I don't know whether I want to laugh or cry. Would you give me some advice on how to deal with these embarrassing situations?

-Amy, Beijing
June 2001

Dear Amy,

Laugh. You can't lower your height, so take it with humor. Tell your roommates you're looking for a boy who's no taller than 140 centimeters, and tell the boys claiming unfairness to get a pair of high-heeled shoes. When people ask how tall you are, ask them why the heck they're so short. People with unusual physiques can often generate supportive laughter simply by being the first to bring up the obvious. Those joke tellers in return get a boost in self-confidence. Eventually, you will believe in your own jokes and stop worrying. Humor can also make you more popular among friends. The comments you mention don't show that people dislike or fear you. They just find your height interesting. After a few jokes, you'll be looking down at smiles on a lot more faces.

Alfred describes pressure to pass exams, but not his own:

Dear Ralph,

I am a university undergraduate. One of my best friends, a cadet in the same city, asked me to help another friend, a cadet who is inept at English, to pass his CET-4 exam (a national standardized English test). I was to take the friend's place by disguising myself as him in the examination room and be the "gunner." She contended that I am the best choice because I have a strong friendship with her and have already passed CET-4. What's more, I am a boy so I can disguise myself as him, unlike my friend. I don't want to lose credit in America, where I'm preparing to go for graduate study, but if I decline, my friend may think I lack loyalty, to which a cadet is especially sensitive. What should I do?
-Alfred, via e-mail
October 2002

Dear Alfred,

Refuse and explain that stepping down serves yourself as well as the real test taker. You already know you have something to lose if caught. But if you succeed, the friend's friend learns nothing. If he can't pass CET-4 himself, how can he continue studying English to pass higher-level exams? What if he later cheats his way into studying in an English-speaking country, then finds he can't communicate abroad, or if he gets a job that requires speaking English? He would be discovered. The discoveries would hurt.

Death, another topic that Chinese generally avoid discussing with family or friends, comes up in one or two letters a year. Someone may ask how to get over a parent who has suddenly died of illness or a workplace accident, reminders that despite China's modernization, health and safety shortfalls often kill people before old age. A few letters also tell of personal suicide plans to escape intractable family problems, study failures or both. Here is the first letter, on any topic, that I answered for the column:

Dear Ralph,

This weekend, as Father's Day comes, many families enjoy themselves in parks or restaurants. However, it's this day that stimulates deep sorrow in my mind, sorrow that involves my father's death. My father was a good man for society. He wasn't able to wake up again when he was hit hard by a motorcycle driven by teenagers on Spring Festival eve. Every day since that accident, or major turn in my life, I have tried to get drunk, especially in school, where I don't want anyone to know my secret. Drinking really seems to be effective. I haven't been derailed from my normal studies. However, as Father's Day comes, I can hardly restrain myself from thinking of the beautiful past and I wonder if I committed suicide whether I would be able to see my great father once more. What else can I do about my love, my sorrow and my memory of him? Please advise me on how to continue my life.

-Pue Kai, Guangdong
June 2000

Dear Pue Kai,

We all get just one father in life. To lose him leaves a big hole where there once was a parent, a friend, a role model and a guide. But forget suicide. You will remain closer to your father by staying alive. What would your dad want for you if he were alive? He would want you to be the best living person possible: studious, charitable, wealthy and self-satisfied. Thinking about this may inspire you to do better for yourself than normal. Save the alcohol for parties. You may be getting by now while drunk, but alcohol is addictive. It eventually makes everything worse. Also, talk about your father with other people. Choose friends who you trust and, patiently, over a few sittings, tell them what happened. Make sure these friends understand how the death affects you long-term so they don't dismiss it by saying something like, "Just get over it." What about your mother and other family members? They are probably affected the same way you are. Deaths sometimes bring survivors closer. Finally, consider carrying on your father's passions. If he collected stamps but was missing a few, for example, finish his collection. This measure should help you understand the man and comfort you by knowing that you're doing something he considered important. If he had no unfinished projects, start one in his honor. For example, put photos of him, any awards he won and things that he wrote into an album titled "Dad."

A letter that hit home

The 21ˢᵗ Century paper pays just eighty Chinese yuan a week for my column. I've outlasted six opinion editors and annual newspaper redesigns. I've held onto the column into 2010, receiving letters and submitting answers through e-mail despite my busy day job. I stick with the column because the Q & A's keep me deep in the trenches of day-to-day China, close to average people's pipedreams, grand schemes, family lives and disasters.

Liberal high school social studies classes and university anthropology lessons had long before taught me not to stand outside a foreign society when there's space inside. I saw the column as part of my obligation to understand China and be almost *one of them* while living in Beijing from mid-1999 through mid-2006.

Chinese people generally believe that no outsider can "get" China, that their long cultural history has placed the race in a unique, unreachable ethno-sphere. China is also globally insulated and hardly multiracial. Communist school texts and state-controlled news media carry messages of Chinese cultural superiority, lest people discover that other countries are ahead economically, politically or in social development. Most people I met in Beijing wanted foreigners to appreciate China but not understand it. Knowing too much comes as a cultural invasion. Foreigners should remain *outside*, where it's safest for China, the thinking goes. As a journalist covering stories about uncompensated property seizures, wrongful incarceration and police beatings, officials who I tried to interview would widen the insider-outsider gap with snarky anti-foreigner remarks or police detention.

But people who write to the column treat me like I belong in their lives. One guy invited me out to an expensive meal of dog meat and vile rice wine during a weekend in his hometown near Beijing. Another letter writer became a beer buddy in Tianjin, where we'd drink the same microbrew and eat the same roast mutton in the same places once every three or four months. We'd share gripes about Internet breakdowns, spotty mobile phone service and the spread of government corruption, or about how our flats were stuck next to twenty-four-hour construction sites half the size of Disneyland. He could have the same discussions with fellow Chinese. As reporter, teacher and columnist in Beijing, I'd hear stories almost daily from someone who had been cheated by a boss, a school or a developer. I tried to help if I had time or knowhow. When I left Beijing, I realized that Chinese people's struggles had become my own.

The tale of Chen Jiaying brought to boil my bonding with China while sharpening the sense I was still unwelcome as a foreigner. It began in 2002, when I was nearing a China fascination peak thanks to my new job at the *South China Morning Post*, where I covered business, entertainment and Beijing, a fast growing city on steroids. I was also teaching journalism part-time at Beijing Broadcasting Institute, where I met more than 250 students. That year Jiaying wrote to the column describing herself as an amateur model who was awkwardly tall for her gender (not the same person who wrote the letter for Chapter 9), especially in her hometown of Changsha, where most people stand five or ten centimeters shorter. Because her letter exceeded my column space, I replied privately, as I often did then, to longer letters. After a few weeks of follow-up emails, I had found out that modeling was only a whim.

"I like a busy life, because idleness make me feel bored to dead, and that's why I became an amateur model before," Jiaying, twenty, wrote at the time. *"I think I should try a lot of fresh things when I am young. When I am old, I can recall my past or tell stories to my progeny."*

More typical of her generation, Jiaying was interested in English, linguistics, the Internet and anything from outside China. Having grown up with open-minded father who once lived abroad, Jiaying never expressed the haughty nationalism or cultural superiority that I often heard around Beijing. This university student would instead offer me hints on how I could teach better at my broadcasting school in Beijing by sharing her own classmates' views on foreign teachers, views from lust to contempt.

Speaking of lust, I never felt any for Jiaying and I doubt she ever did for me. It's important to point that out given what happened later.

We became friends. When Jiaying picked me up at the Changsha railway depot in September 2002 to show me around town, she said my arrival proved that Internet friendship wasn't always a fraud as her mother had feared. There I was offline at the appointed time and place, without thugs or sidearms. Later that day at Jiaying's family apartment I saw the cement walls and floors of standard housing for state workers such as her parents. After a home-cooked lunch heavy on chili peppers (mild ones for the foreigner, it was explained), I witnessed an example of the power outages common outside Beijing due to overuse of electricity and distribution problems. Jiaying's father did not blow his fuse. He gave me a be-patient-with-developing-China speech. But I could tell from his suppressed smirk that he was speaking pro forma, as most Chinese do with foreigners when things go wrong. He was pissed.

Jiaying barely noticed. "You mentioned your middle school years. They sound mysterious; I'm going to dig out some secrets when you pass out, then write a news story and publish it," she wrote in an e-mail later reflecting the tone of our trip. Ji-aying continued contributing to my intensive self-study of China by answering questions that other friends found sensitive or embarrassing. For example, when too many of my students were seeking my help on complex study-abroad applications but I wasn't sure if I should turn some away, Jiaying wrote:

"I don't think you should do everything for them, just give them some suggestions, because I find that when students know a teacher is kind, they will always try to take advantage of him. I know you are very busy, and it seems you are a working machine sometimes. I don't mean you shouldn't give your students a hand, but not too much. I mean there's a limit, and if you exceed a certain limit, then you are going to spoil them. Here, our foreign teachers don't do that extra work, and students don't make such demands. Maybe there are some extra demands, but I don't see them, because most of that would be done under the table. You get it?"

I guess I didn't get it, because I agreed to proofread Jiaying's own thesis on psycholinguistics in 2003. It was full of long, un-attributed, grammatically flawless passages alternating with her own decent but still clearly non-native English. I asked Jiaying what she had plagiarized. Copying excerpts isn't plagiarism, she said, reflecting how many of my own students regarded their journalism homework.

"I didn't plagiarize sentence by sentence. I mixed other material together with my words," she wrote. "I should be frank that I did copy some materials as grounds for my argument. I looked up many books, read many magazines and newspapers, and browsed many web pages to collect material. But (the conclusion) is myself, so the expressions in this chapter sound more like Jiaying language."

Challenging her thesis was my first mistake. One day in 2004 Jiaying suddenly came to Beijing. "My parents don't know what I'm up to here and don't tell them," she said, "but where is the Pakistani embassy?" She needed a visa to visit her Internet boyfriend in Lahore. Mom and Pop knew nothing about the boyfriend. Otherwise they would have chained her to a cement wall. I helped Jiaying find a budget Beijing hotel, treated her to a few meals and showed her around town as she had done for me in Changhsha. In a week she got a visa and went to Lahore. Her parents still didn't know.

Days after she left China, her dad sent me a mobile phone text message asking what I knew. I told him the story and offered that Jiaying might be short of call-home time while getting settled in Pakistan. She had actually stayed quiet for fear of parental outrage. Her mother later called to ask that I file a missing-person report with the Pakistani embassy and to dial the only Lahore telephone number that she could find after raiding Jiaying's e-mails. I did both, but no results. Ten days later, Jiaying called home.

Two months after that, she returned to Changsha and married the Pakistani boyfriend. Both found jobs teaching English at the same university there and shared a flat. In 2005 he took a liking to other women on campus. Jiaying asked for a divorce. Divorce in China shames the couple and their families. It's especially hard when the woman is just twenty-three. It's even harder when a marriage lasts for less than a year and harder yet when it ends with a man's designs to cheat. Since the story concerns China, we must loudly reiterate that the aggressor here was a foreigner, whose ilk is already stereotyped over its lack of concern for family unity. Jiaying detailed the pending divorce for me, hitting hard at the shame element and at the students who went after her mate.

She spent much of 2005 avoiding old friends so they wouldn't gossip about her. She expressed little interest in new Internet friendships. The only child went back to live with her parents and spent their money but got away with declining an easy job in her father's government office. She applied for a linguistics graduate program in the Netherlands but didn't qualify.

Meanwhile, her mom went mad over the divorce, telling Jiaying, "I told you so" as often as possible while resolving to stop anything else like it from happening.

"My parents took away my ID card, my passport, my deposits, everything concerning (ex-husband) Rizwan and deleted pictures from my computer," Jiaying wrote to me. "They stop giving me even a penny now, and I rely on the coins that I can steal when they're not home."

Mom invited a series of locally employed, financially stable, boring and, of course, Chinese men to eat together with the family, hoping Jiaying would go for one. Jiaying went for none.

"The little uncle is not a bad person indeed, but I was against my mom and treated him unfairly," she wrote after one suitor had gone his own way in early 2006. "He had found his woman earlier, and just few days ago, I invited him out to apologize for my previous rude behavior toward him. I said everything clearly and told him exactly what I thought. By the way, I asked him to persuade my mom to take it easy. Anyway, it's not a bad that we are friends now. Whew!"

Jiaying also told the folks she was still writing to me after long concealing our e-mails and text messages to head off a suspicion that I had a role in the failed marriage. In early 2006 her dad sent me a text message demanding that I sever all contact with Jiaying but not tell her why. Instead I contacted him. My wife, who had met Jiaying before she left for Pakistan, went on the call to explain that we saw her as an adventurous friend who I intended to keep. Her father said he didn't object but that his wife had put him up to sending me the text message. She figured that as an

American I had led Jiaying to foreign temptations ending in the divorce. "If not for you," her mother once asked me, "why else would she care about all this nonsense outside China?"

A new parent-proof e-mail account helped Jiaying and me keep a line open. But she must have let something else slip, because her mother texted me a few months later asking that I not meet with her daughter. I wrote back that I had no plans to meet.

Jiaying was accepted to a linguistics graduate program in New Delhi that year. Before she left the country again, we met in a city where I was doing a weekend reporting assignment. During our lunch there, her mother texted me again asking that I avoid Jiaying, who told me to ignore it.

Since she moved to New Delhi and I to Taipei in 2006, I've gotten e-mails but nothing like before. We both have a lineup of new friends. Neither of us wants more strife in her family. She seldom mentions her parents, their orders against me, the hacked e-mails or the ex-husband. When I asked her once to reflect on the past, she sent this e-mail a few months into her first semester in New Delhi:

"I am hardly online, because real life is much busier and more interesting than cyber life. Luckily, I haven't dated any Indians till now, but I've found them annoying sometimes. I am staying with foreign friends most of the time. I have a very nice friend from Iran in my hostel, and we usually go out and travel together. You know I've come here for not finding a boy but to enjoy my own life. I think as long as I am happy, why need a boy to bother me? I might get hurt at last again. So I choose to be whatever I feel is comfortable, and let's see who will catch me finally."

IN CLOSING

Chen Jiaying is clearly no isolated case in China. Jiaying's peers across the country socialize largely in the cozy, scripted Internet environment so they can meet anyone from anywhere without feeling nervous or leaving home against the will of parents. Those peers often work, as Jiaying did, toward getting into master's degree programs at foreign universities. In China, they cheat on all or part of their term papers and exams. Foreign boyfriends are in demand among Jiaying's female Chinese contemporaries seeking adventure, global experience or money.

Jiaying's graduation, disappearance in Pakistan, reemergence at home in China, marriage, divorce, voluntary unemployment and departure for India—all within four years—reflect her generation's fixation on fast change, much of it hollow and poorly planned, a byproduct of China's competitive get-ahead-quick ethos.

My friend's liberal, relaxed but cautious father and her xenophobic, traditional, panicked mother can claim plenty of peers, too. On the defensive against the unknown, they commonly try to squelch whatever ambitions might lead their child outside China or even outside their hometown. Impacted by the 1966-76 Cultural Revolution, a decade when neighbors publicly humiliated one another for having money and then took away one another's property, all with government approval, parents tend to distrust strangers without a trial period. Foreigners are about the strangest. According to today's official textbooks and mass media, people outside China are culturally crude and politically untrustworthy. But some mothers and fathers nevertheless hope their children marry into developed countries for the money that a foreign spouse might bring into the family. And like Jiaying's father, a growing number of parents reject government propaganda, even preferring the company of foreigners to Chinese people who are stuck in the dog-eat-dogma rat race of their fast developing nation.

Elders all over China still play matchmaker, per cultural habit, for their children as if they were wall sockets that just need the right plug. Matchmaking intensifies after a child's own failures, such as Jiaying's divorce. Her mother simply saw it as her Confucian duty to protect and control Jiaying for as long into her adulthood as necessary. Finally, Mom and Dad did what people their age often do when someone under them gets out of line: an authoritative crackdown. Her parents figured they could cut off Jiaying's social life without negotiating, because they were ultimately in charge.

Jiaying and both parents hid truths about their desires or intentions. Indirect communication permeates every strata of China. Infatuated women seldom level with the objects of their desire. Co-workers settle office disputes with silent treatment or backstabbing. Young Chinese say they appreciate honesty when they find it, but few of them speak frankly.

Finally, Jiaying's story shows what can happen when foreigners get involved. Jiaying was excited to leave China, express non-Chinese ideas and use English with non-Chinese people. She had no idea that she'd fight for years, losing her ID and e-mail privacy, to get the foreign experience she wanted without breaking diplomatic ties at home.

In mid-2009, Jiaying returned to China from India with a master's degree. After living at home again for a while, she moved to the southern Chinese city of Guangzhou to work in trade using connections with foreigners who she met in New Delhi. She's engaged to marry one of them.

www.ingramcontent.com/pod-product-compliance
Lightning Source LLC
Chambersburg PA
CBHW071250280526
45788CB00004B/1662